Table of Contents

Note: *The authors acknowledge the research and writing contributions of Robert Gonyea, Julie Williams, and John Kuykendall, all of Indiana University, to this text.*

The authors acknowledge the contributions to this text by the advance review team of Larry Roper, of Oregon State University; Barbara Snyder, of the University of Utah; and Marilee Bresciani, of Texas A&M University.

Introduction

This guide is intended to help academic and student life administrators, faculty members, and others use knowledge about how students' expectations shape their college experiences in order to improve the quality of undergraduate education. To illustrate how student expectations may vary across different types of colleges and universities, we present four case examples from institutions with different missions, along with an analysis of what each institution might do to change its policies and practices in ways that would promote student engagement and success. Then, we offer sets of questions institutions can use to more accurately determine what their students expect from college and how the institutions can appropriately respond in the following areas: learning and academic achievement; college life and environment; student services, cost, persistence and educational attainment; and outcomes of the college experience.

The expectations of constituents beyond the campus community are also relevant to creating learning environments that meet students' and societal needs. Toward that end, we review expectations that various groups have for undergraduate education including parents and families, communities and local government, alumni and donors, and employers.

Our intention is that this guide be used in tandem with the book *Promoting Reasonable Expectations: Aligning Student and Institutional Views of the College Experience* (Miller, Bender, Schuh, & Associates, 2005) to inform discussions about student and institutional expectations, design assessments of relevant student experiences and school conditions, and point to policies and practices that institutions can create or modify to enhance student learning and educational effectiveness.

History

The Reasonable Expectations project was prompted by the 25th anniversary and re-issue of the *Joint Statement of Rights and Freedoms of Students* by the American Association of University Professors (American Association of University Professors, 1968). Following the publication of the 1992 version, leaders of the National Association of Student

Personnel Administrators (NASPA) hosted a series of conversations about the relevance and applications of the *Joint Statement.* Clearly, protecting the rights of students in every era is a necessary condition for creating an appropriate climate for learning. Out of these discussions emerged the sense that the nature of student-institutional relations had become confused, even counterproductive, due to a confluence of factors.

In the summer of 1993, the NASPA Board of Directors commissioned a writing team to clarify the desired relationships between students and institutions of higher learning with an eye toward improving student learning and educational effectiveness. At the core of the discussion was the matter of what students expect of higher education and what, in turn, institutions expect of students. George Kuh (Indiana University), James Lyons (Stanford University), Jo Anne Trow (Oregon State University), and Thomas Miller (Canisius College) met several times over a two-year period. The product of their work was *Reasonable Expectations* (National Association of Student Personnel Administrators, 1994), a document that spawned a series of workshops and programs at conferences and on college campuses that further examined the implications of clearly communicating what students could expect from their college or university and what institutions could reasonably expect from students.

The *Reasonable Expectations* pamphlet provided a lens through which a variety of relevant student-institution relationships could be viewed. Five categories of expectations were explicated: teaching and learning, the curriculum, institutional integrity, the quality of institutional life, and educational services. A sampling of expectations within each category illustrated areas where the interactions between students and their institution could be clarified in order to improve the educational experience.

In the years that followed, NASPA hosted various workshops and programs around the student expectations theme. Also, there was some interest in the higher educational research community about student expectations. In the fall of 2002, the NASPA Board of Directors authorized the appointment of a group to revisit the role, relevance, and impact of *Reasonable Expectations.* A design team, comprised of the following persons, was convened:

Barbara Bender, *Rutgers University*
Evelyn Clements, *Middlesex Community College*
George Kuh, *Indiana University*
Thomas Miller, *University of South Florida*
Gregory Roberts, *University of St. Thomas*
John Schuh, *Iowa State University*

The product of their work, which drew on the talents and perspectives of many other persons, was *Promoting Reasonable Expectations: Aligning Student and Institutional Views of the College Experience* (Miller, et al., 2005). This volume underscored the dissonance between student expectations and their subsequent experiences, based upon national research and broad studies. As such, it set the stage for this guide, which provides a framework practitioners and scholars can use to explore student expectations and apply the principles discussed in *Promoting Reasonable Expectations*. Our purpose here is to encourage and support efforts to better understand students' expectations for college, and to take action to reduce the discrepancies between what students and institutions want from one another.

Why Should We Take Student Expectations Seriously?

Students' expectations for college matter because they form the foundation for the nature of the relationship students have with their college or university. As with most relationships, each party presumes the other will act and respond in certain ways for the relationship to be mutually beneficial. When these expectations are not met, one or both parties must adjust their expectations lest they become very dissatisfied. In the worst case, relationships are terminated. Such may be the case when many students leave college prematurely (Miller, 2005).

Expectations are created out of a melding of past experiences in anticipation of some desired future state of affairs (Arnold & Kuh, 1999; Howard, 2005; Kelly, 1955; Rousseau, 2001). Students entering college base their expectations on various sources of information—what parents and siblings have said, how media and popular culture portray the college experience, their past experiences with educational institutions, the admissions process, and their own impressions of how they compare to their college-bound peers. It stands to reason that when college faculty members and administrators have good information about what their students expect, they will be better prepared to design learning environments that challenge and support students at appropriate levels.

During the past 20 years, increased attention has been given to the importance of the first year of college. Research indicates that student success has much to do with these initial experiences in the first few weeks of college (Upcraft, Gardner, Barefoot & Associates, 2005). The premise of the study of expectations suggests that these experiences may be influenced by the expectations students bring to the table. In some cases, expectations may be unreasonable and may require re-educating and informing students of what they can expect in given situations within the college environment. In other situations, student expectations may be quite on-target, and the onus is on the institution to make sure these expectations are being met.

Psychological and cognitive factors such as student aspirations, motivation, ability, and positive orientation to college appear to influence student expectations to varying degrees.

Student demographics such as race, sex, and socioeconomic status matter less. In addition, institutional characteristics provide little understanding for predicting expectations. This suggests that regardless of size, location, mission, or status, colleges and universities have the ability to form and shape expectations after accounting for student aspirations, ability, and motivation (Kuh, Gonyea, & Williams, 2005).

In order to meet student expectations, we first must understand their expectations. This requires study and assessment at the institutional level. While some normative data exist that can serve to guide our assumptions about student expectations, each institution must measure these expectations in light of its own mission, purpose, and values. Additionally, schools must explore whether students with diverse background characteristics have different expectations for their college experience. Differences in gender, race, and age may all influence the expectations that students hold (Dungy, Rissmeyer, & Roberts, 2005). The closer an institution can get to matching the experience of students with their expectations, the more likely it is that students will desire to continue the relationship and remain enrolled at the institution (Braxton, Hossler, & Vesper, 1995).

Assessment Approaches

There are many ways an institution can gather the data needed to explore and analyze student expectations. As the applications described in the following section indicate, the *College Student Expectations Questionnaire* (CSXQ) (Kuh & Pace, 1999) is designed to gather information about student expectations prior to their matriculation. Collecting data about expectations allows administrators and faculty members to consider program and instruction adjustments that respond to student beliefs about what they will encounter in college. It also permits institutional personnel to consider strategies for reframing student expectations when they are determined to be unreasonable.

The CSXQ, when combined with its sister instrument, the *College Student Experiences Questionnaire* (CSEQ) (Pace & Kuh, 1998), enables institutions to compare what students expect from college with their subsequent experiences on the same basic set of considerations regarding in-class and out-of-class behaviors. CSXQ asks students how often they expect to engage in the important learning activities appearing on the CSEQ, and asks them to estimate how much emphasis the institution will place on various learning tasks and goals. Of the research tools available to study expectations and experiences of students, the CSXQ and CSEQ tools, when used together, are the most directly relevant.

As described in *Promoting Reasonable Expectations* (Miller, et al., 2005), the Cooperative Institutional Research Program (CIRP) (Sax, Lindholm, Astin, Korn, & Mahoney, 2002) is another appropriate instrument for assessing student expectations. It is generally administered before matriculation or shortly thereafter. CIRP has value beyond the measure of expectations, because it more broadly surveys students about their attitudes, experiences, values, and backgrounds. Although it has that important advantage, its study of expectations is not as thorough as the CSXQ.

Another tool under development that schools can consider is the *Beginning College Survey of Student Engagement* (BCSSE) (2005), which is designed to be paired with the widely used National Survey of Student Engagement (NSSE) (2006) (http://www.nsse.iub.edu/pdf/BCSSE_2005_Sample.pdf). The BCSSE is the precollege companion to NSSE, and focuses on entering first-year students' high school academic and extracurricular involvements as well as on the importance that students ascribe to their participation in educationally purposeful activities during the first college year.

Nationally normed instruments have many advantages. At the same time, locally developed tools may also be useful. What is lost with the latter is the ability to compare institutional results with national norms, but what is gained is focused and well-targeted research. Institutions that develop their own research instruments can study specific institutional aspects of the student experience and consider unique cultural and organizational characteristics. Further, much can be gained from qualitative research, interviewing students, and sponsoring focus groups.

Interviewing students as part of academic advising, career planning experiences, or other individual encounters with students yields instructive information. When students are individually engaged in conversations about their expectations, the research applications may be modest, but the opportunity to personally negotiate expectations and help the student develop reasonable ones is an effective tool for improving the relationships between students and institutions.

Any approach used to compare student expectations and experiences must have a broad base of institutional support. Little will be accomplished with data about student expectations if the purpose of the inquiry is not understood and the results welcomed and widely disseminated. If these conditions are not cultivated, there is no reason to believe substantive, sustained changes in institutional policies and practices will follow. In the next section, we illustrate some of what can be learned from assessing student expectations and experiences, and how institutions can use this information to improve the quality of the student experience.

Using Data About College Expectations & Experiences to Guide Improvement Efforts

First-year students generally have higher expectations for themselves and the academic demands of college than what they subsequently experience (Kuh, Gonyea, & Williams, 2005). That is, they start college thinking they will study more, read and write more, and spend more time with faculty than they report doing during their first college year.

The expected and reported levels of engagement vary in predictable ways by institutional type (Astin, 1993; Kuh 2005). For example, students at smaller, selective, residential colleges have greater expectations across the board. Near the end of the first year of college, they report having been involved to a greater extent in more activities than students at other types of colleges and universities. They also, on average, expect and find their campus environments to be more supportive. At the same time, some large schools outperform some small schools on these dimensions (National Survey of Student Engagement, 2001, 2004).

Although students expect to do more in college than they actually do, their expectations for participating in a variety of academic and intellectual activities seem reasonable. In fact, they are generally consistent with what faculty members assert is a necessary level of academic effort in terms of amount of reading and writing. Faculty members expect students to study about two hours for every class hour, which is more than twice as much as students report studying. But when pressed, faculty admit that their own students spend an hour or less preparing for class. All this raises some questions about the amount and nature of academic work assigned, and the nature and range of intellectual skills required to produce the academic work at an acceptable level of quality. As Olsen et al. (1998, p. 18) observed from their study of Indiana University Bloomington students:

> *Students read, but only required texts and rarely primary sources or non-assigned books. Students wrote, but their writing activities emphasized grammar and word usage as contrasted with integration and synthesis. The small fraction of students who were engaged in science activities tended to memorize formulas and definitions and rarely used the scientific method for problem solving. Students talked often with faculty members, but their conversations tended to focus on the organizational*

details of classes rather than more substantive questions about course content and learning. Students studied, but they used primarily passive study strategies.

The gap between expectations and experiences also extends to social life beyond the classroom (Kuh, 2005). Compared with previous generations, students today are less disposed to join campus-based organizations, to participate in formally organized social events, to get involved in student government, to use the campus union, or to attend cultural or performing arts events. They are more inclined toward spontaneous, informal social interaction with peers (Kuh, 1999; Levine & Cureton, 1998).

Of course, more than a few students do take advantage of the many learning opportunities their schools provide. Olsen et al. (1998) found that better academically prepared students were more engaged in college. That is, those who had high class ranks and grades and who took more English courses studied more in college and were more involved in a variety of educationally purposeful activities.

Even so, many students are "disengaged" from the learning process (Kuh, 2003, p. 27; Levine & Cureton, 1998). A substantial proportion may not fully understand and appreciate their role as learners. For example, they may not be able or know how to process information at deep, meaningful levels or be developmentally ready to use higher order thinking skills. Also, when faculty members expect students to do certain things and then devote class time or assign students out-of-class work related to these tasks, students by and large do them and benefit more from college than their peers who do not engage in these or other purposeful activities to the same degree (Kuh, Nelson Laird, & Umbach, 2004). This suggests that faculty members and student affairs professionals must clearly and consistently communicate to students what is expected and provide periodic feedback as to the quality of students' performance. According to English professor Richard Turner (1998, p. 4):

> *...success in college may have more to do with introducing [students] to academic citizenship within their course work than with expanded orientations or increased access to information resources. [Professors must] explain things which professors never used to have to explain to students—you must buy the book, you must read it and come to class, you must observe deadlines or make special arrangements when you miss one.*

Good Things Go Together

This brief summary of first-year student expectations and college experiences suggests that institutions need to better understand their students and the nature of their activities during college. As Tables 1.1-4 (below) show, students at different types of institutions who participate more frequently in various educationally purposeful activities benefit more in desired areas. For example, students who frequently work on projects that require integrating ideas report making greater gains in synthesizing ideas. Similarly, students at all colleges who contribute frequently to class discussions gain more in speaking effectively; those who work often on class projects with peers believe they gain more in their ability to work effectively as a team member. This pattern holds across the board—from community colleges to selective private residential colleges to large public universities. Indeed, the strong positive relationship between student engagement and college outcomes is well documented (Astin, 1993; Pascarella & Terenzini, 2005).

Table 1.1 Western State College Gains

Working with others on class projects	**Gain: Speaking effectively**		
	Very Little	Some	Substantial
Never	12%	5%	2%
Occasionally	42%	37%	22%
Frequently	46%	58%	76%

Putting together different facts and ideas	**Gain: Synthesizing Ideas**		
	Very Little	Some	Substantial
Never	21%	8%	3%
Occasionally	41%	44%	26%
Frequently	39%	48%	71%

Working on projects that integrate ideas from various sources	**Gain: Writing effectively**		
	Very Little	Some	Substantial
Never	10%	4%	1%
Occasionally	39%	33%	19%
Frequently	51%	63%	80%

Discussing current events in the news outside of class	**Gain: Knowledge about the world**		
	Very Little	Some	Substantial
Never	5%	3%	2%
Occasionally	44%	39%	28%
Frequently	51%	59%	70%

Table 1.1 continued

		Gain: Knowledge about the world		
		Very Little	Some	Substantial
Discussing social issues (peace, justice, etc.) outside of class	Never	16%	9%	5%
	Occasionally	50%	49%	35%
	Frequently	34%	43%	60%

		Gain: Speaking effectively		
		Very Little	Some	Substantial
Contributing to class discussions	Never	10%	4%	2%
	Occasionally	46%	43%	26%
	Frequently	43%	53%	72%

		Gain: Functioning as a team member		
		Very Little	Some	Substantial
Working with others on class projects	Never	13%	6%	2%
	Occasionally	46%	40%	22%
	Frequently	41%	54%	76%

		Gain: Consequences of science, tech.		
		Very Little	Some	Substantial
Discussing social/ethical issues related to science outside of class	Never	39%	22%	11%
	Occasionally	44%	54%	41%
	Frequently	17%	24%	48%

		Gain: Thinking analytically		
		Very Little	Some	Substantial
Putting together different facts and ideas	Never	17%	7%	3%
	Occasionally	43%	43%	26%
	Frequently	40%	50%	71%

Table 1.2 Pristine Pond College Gains

		Gain: Speaking effectively		
		Very Little	Some	Substantial
Working with others on class projects	Never	8%	4%	2%
	Occasionally	50%	41%	27%
	Frequently	42%	55%	71%

		Gain: Synthesizing Ideas		
		Very Little	Some	Substantial
Putting together different facts and ideas	Never	9%	4%	1%
	Occasionally	30%	31%	12%
	Frequently	61%	65%	88%

		Gain: Writing effectively		
		Very Little	Some	Substantial
Working on projects that integrate ideas from various sources	Never	10%	3%	1%
	Occasionally	40%	30%	14%
	Frequently	49%	68%	85%

		Gain: Knowledge about the world		
		Very Little	Some	Substantial
Discussing current events in the news outside of class	Never	5%	2%	1%
	Occasionally	46%	39%	27%
	Frequently	50%	59%	72%

		Gain: Knowledge about the world		
		Very Little	Some	Substantial
Discussing social issues (peace, justice, etc.) outside of class	Never	10%	5%	2%
	Occasionally	49%	42%	26%
	Frequently	41%	53%	72%

		Gain: Speaking effectively		
		Very Little	Some	Substantial
Contributing to class discussions	Never	9%	2%	1%
	Occasionally	43%	35%	20%
	Frequently	48%	63%	79%

Table 1.2 continued

Working with others on class projects	**Gain: Functioning as a team member**		
	Very Little	Some	Substantial
Never	12%	4%	2%
Occasionally	51%	43%	25%
Frequently	37%	53%	74%

Discussing social/ethical issues related to science outside of class	**Gain: Consequences of science, tech**		
	Very Little	Some	Substantial
Never	27%	13%	5%
Occasionally	50%	52%	34%
Frequently	23%	36%	60%

Putting together different facts and ideas	**Gain: Thinking analytically**		
	Very Little	Some	Substantial
Never	8%	3%	1%
Occasionally	28%	28%	12%
Frequently	65%	69%	87%

Table 1.3 University of the Great Plains Gains

Working with others on class projects	**Gain: Speaking effectively**		
	Very Little	Some	Substantial
Never	11%	6%	3%
Occasionally	45%	40%	26%
Frequently	44%	55%	71%

Putting together different facts and ideas	**Gain: Synthesizing Ideas**		
	Very Little	Some	Substantial
Never	12%	5%	2%
Occasionally	36%	37%	18%
Frequently	52%	57%	80%

Working on projects that integrate ideas from various sources	**Gain: Writing effectively**		
	Very Little	Some	Substantial
Never	12%	4%	2%
Occasionally	36%	34%	18%
Frequently	52%	61%	81%

Table 1.3 continued

	Gain: Knowledge about the world		
		Very Little	Some	Substantial
Discussing current events in the news outside of class	Never	4%	2%	2%
	Occasionally	41%	35%	24%
	Frequently	55%	63%	74%

	Gain: Knowledge about the world		
		Very Little	Some	Substantial
Discussing social issues (peace, justice, etc.) outside of class	Never	13%	6%	3%
	Occasionally	49%	45%	30%
	Frequently	39%	49%	66%

	Gain: Speaking effectively		
		Very Little	Some	Substantial
Contributing to class discussions	Never	10%	4%	2%
	Occasionally	44%	41%	26%
	Frequently	47%	55%	72%

	Gain: Functioning as a team member		
		Very Little	Some	Substantial
Working with others on class projects	Never	16%	6%	3%
	Occasionally	50%	45%	24%
	Frequently	34%	50%	73%

	Gain: Consequences of science, tech.		
		Very Little	Some	Substantial
Discussing social/ethical issues related to science outside of class	Never	34%	17%	8%
	Occasionally	46%	54%	39%
	Frequently	20%	30%	53%

	Gain: Thinking analytically		
		Very Little	Some	Substantial
Putting together different facts and ideas	Never	12%	5%	2%
	Occasionally	36%	36%	18%
	Frequently	52%	59%	80%

Table 1.4 Atlantic County Community College Gains

Working with others on class projects	Gain: Speaking effectively		
	Very Little	Some	Substantial
Never	19%	9%	5%
Occasionally	47%	40%	26%
Frequently	34%	51%	69%

Putting together different facts and ideas	Gain: Synthesizing Ideas		
	Very Little	Some	Substantial
Never	24%	7%	8%
Occasionally	27%	46%	28%
Frequently	49%	47%	65%

Working on projects that integrate ideas from various sources	Gain: Writing effectively		
	Very Little	Some	Substantial
Never	13%	7%	1%
Occasionally	32%	31%	20%
Frequently	55%	63%	78%

Discussing current events in the news outside of class	Gain: Knowledge about the world		
	Very Little	Some	Substantial
Never	5%	3%	4%
Occasionally	28%	31%	18%
Frequently	67%	66%	78%

Discussing social issues (peace, justice, etc.) outside of class	Gain: Knowledge about the world		
	Very Little	Some	Substantial
Never	14%	10%	6%
Occasionally	36%	41%	28%
Frequently	51%	49%	66%

Contributing to class discussions	Gain: Speaking effectively		
	Very Little	Some	Substantial
Never	22%	6%	1%
Occasionally	34%	36%	20%
Frequently	44%	58%	79%

Table 1.4 continued

Working with others on class projects	Gain: Functioning as a team member		
	Very Little	Some	Substantial
Never	27%	9%	5%
Occasionally	39%	41%	27%
Frequently	33%	50%	68%

Discussing social/ethical issues related to science outside of class	Gain: Consequences of science, tech.		
	Very Little	Some	Substantial
Never	36%	23%	16%
Occasionally	36%	50%	37%
Frequently	28%	27%	47%

Putting together different facts and ideas	Gain: Thinking analytically		
	Very Little	Some	Substantial
Never	23%	12%	5%
Occasionally	36%	43%	27%
Frequently	41%	45%	68%

Student engagement and educational effectiveness at most colleges and universities would improve if schools embarked on a comprehensive strategic approach to discover what students expect to do during the first year of college, and then design learning activities and out-of-class events that require or induce students to meet these high expectations. As with most matters related to institutional improvement, the devil is in the details. It's one thing to be aware of general trends, but quite another to know exactly where to start to work on one's campus. Institutional mission, size, student characteristics, and nature of the educational program all must be taken into account. Equally important are trustworthy, reliable data to confirm suspicions, mobilize action, and prioritize interventions.

A Tale of Four Campuses

To illustrate how information about student expectations and experiences can be used to guide improvement efforts, we use vignettes from four different types of institutions. The schools and their data are real, though we've assigned them pseudonyms. While the general pattern described earlier holds for all of the schools—students are less engaged overall than they expected to be—the examples tell somewhat different stories about what students who matriculate to the respective institution expect, and what they actually do and get out of the first year of college. As a result, the kinds of policies and programs that might have desired effects will differ some from one school to another.

For each institution, we offer several suggestions for what faculty and staff could do to begin to address the institutional factors and student behaviors that are likely contributing to the results. These are not the only actions that might have the desired effects, but they illustrate the kinds of things faculty, staff, and others can consider to close the gap between expectations and experiences and enhance collegiate quality.

Western State College

Western State College (WSC) is part of a state system west of the Mississippi. Classified as a Master's I institution by The Carnegie Foundation for the Advancement of Teaching (2001), it enrolls more than 20,000 students, most of whom are undergraduates. Its Barron's (College Division of Barron's Educational Series, 2002) selectivity index is three, or competitive, which means that most of the students who apply are admitted. Only about 5% live in campus housing, most of whom are first-year students.

In general, the expectations of WSC first-year students are consistent with the general finding that students' precollege expectations are greater than experiences. For example, as Table 2.1 shows, students expected to interact more frequently with students from different backgrounds (age, race/ethnicity) and with different interests than they actually did. They also expected to read more than they did (Table 2.1 below).

At the same time, it is noteworthy that WSC appears to be doing some things that result in students exceeding their expectations in some important areas, such as using information from other areas of their life in class discussions, explaining course material, talking about current events, and integrating ideas into their papers and other course projects.

Table 2.1 Western State College Frequencies

		CSXQ	CSEQ
Contributing to class discussions	never	5%	5%
	occasionally	39%	34%
	frequently	57%	61%
Applying class material to other areas (job, relationships, etc.)	never	3%	2%
	occasionally	28%	18%
	frequently	68%	79%
Using a campus learning lab or center	never	26%	59%
	occasionally	40%	26%
	frequently	34%	15%
Becoming acquainted with students of different backgrounds	never	2%	3%
	occasionally	26%	30%
	frequently	72%	66%
Number of essays written	none	2%	7%
	fewer than 5	17%	30%
	between 5 and 10	31%	32%
	between 10 and 20	33%	22%
	more than 20	17%	8%
Student rating: Extent to which campus emphasizes diversity	Low (1,2)	2%	7%
	Middle (3,4,5)	46%	50%
	High (6,7)	52%	43%
Using information from other areas of life in class	never	4%	3%
	occasionally	31%	23%
	frequently	66%	74%
Explaining course material to others	never	4%	2%
	occasionally	35%	18%
	frequently	61%	80%
Working on projects integrating ideas from various sources	never	4%	2%
	occasionally	28%	12%
	frequently	68%	86%

Table 2.1 continued

		CSXQ	CSEQ
Becoming acquainted with students of a different age	never	1%	3%
	occasionally	21%	26%
	frequently	78%	71%
Serious discussions with students of different race	never	13%	15%
	occasionally	34%	39%
	frequently	53%	46%
Explaining scientific concept to others	never	19%	18%
	occasionally	45%	37%
	frequently	36%	45%
Discussing current events in the news outside of class	never	8%	2%
	occasionally	38%	29%
	frequently	54%	69%
Discussing social issues (peace, justice, etc.) outside of class	never	13%	8%
	occasionally	47%	38%
	frequently	40%	53%
Discussing different lifestyles, customs, and religions outside of class	never	9%	7%
	occasionally	42%	37%
	frequently	50%	57%
Discussing the ideas of writers, philosophers, historians outside of class	never	31%	22%
	occasionally	46%	45%
	frequently	24%	33%
Discussing science (theories, experiments, methods) outside of class	never	41%	28%
	occasionally	39%	40%
	frequently	20%	32%
Discussing social/ethical issues related to science outside of class	never	24%	14%
	occasionally	47%	45%
	frequently	30%	41%
Number of texts read	none	0%	4%
	fewer than 5	13%	37%
	between 5 and 10	42%	40%
	between 10 and 20	31%	15%
	more than 20	14%	4%

These affirming findings suggest the learning communities that WSC has introduced may be having the desired effects. About 20% of first-year students are co-enrolled in two courses, one of which is the gateway writing course that is a general education requirement.

Instructors of the two courses are encouraged to develop assignments and course activities that require students to draw on readings and course activities from both classes. Because participating in learning communities is linked to a constellation of desired outcomes—including persistence (Taylor, Moore, MacGregor, & Lindblad, 2003; Tinto, 2000; Zhao & Kuh, 2004)—WSC's goal is to increase the number of learning communities so that more than half of the incoming class each year, about 2,800 students, will begin college as members of a learning community, which creates social networks using the classroom as the locus of community-building. This is especially important for commuter students who spend less time on campus and interact less with their peers inside and outside the classroom.

The learning community initiative at WSC also seems to be having additional salutary effects on other aspects of the first-year experience. For example, the active and collaborative learning practices adopted by many of the instructors of learning community courses are being tried by other faculty members, especially colleagues teaching other general educational courses subscribed to primarily by first-year students.

Higher education is obligated to prepare students from different backgrounds to live and work in a diverse society (Hurtado, Milem, Clayton-Pedersen, & Allen, 1999; Umbach & Kuh, in press). To its credit, WSC recognizes that experiencing diversity is a significant educational resource. Therefore, administrators are seeking ways to promote substantive interactions between students of different racial and ethnic backgrounds, as these experiences are associated with enhanced learning and personal development. One reason it's especially important to foster interactions between people from different backgrounds in the first year of college is that the frequency of such contacts decreases over time as students move through college (Hu & Kuh, 2003). In large part, this is because students are more likely to live off campus after the first year.

After considering a variety of options, WSC is considering placing additional emphasis on diversity during orientation, and reinforcing this with a multicultural component in the required writing course that is part of the learning community. This will include at least one writing assignment that features some aspect of human diversity. In addition, WSC is considering requiring a course on multiculturalism to be completed after the first year of college as part of the general education sequence, and participation in a minimum number of events on campus that will expose students to different cultures.

Another step WSC might consider is making sure early warning systems and redundant safety nets are working well to identify students who are struggling or who are underengaged early in the first academic term. It's generally too late to wait until mid-term grades are distributed to advisors and students to help students salvage a poor semester. Academic advisors and support program personnel at Truman State, for example, used Student

Advising Reports derived from CSEQ data to help students see how their in-class and out-of-class activities compare with those of their peers in terms of study time, talking with faculty members about various matters, and participation in cocurricular activities, to name a few. Other schools using the Student Advising Reports in the last two years include Marietta College, Illinois State University, University of South Carolina Upstate, Rocky Mountain College, University of Evansville, and Saint Mary's University-San Antonio.

Pristine Pond College

Pristine Pond College (PPC) is a small, selective, independent liberal arts college in the Northeast with about 1,300 students, virtually all of whom are of traditional age, attend full-time, and live on campus. Situated on the edge of a small town about a two-hour drive from the nearest metropolitan area, more than half of the students are from out of state. There are, however, almost a dozen colleges and universities within a 50-mile radius. Tuition and fees, including room and board, are close to $40,000. The Barron's selectivity index is six, making PPC one of the 150 or so most selective schools in the country.

As with other selective liberal arts colleges, PPC's students arrive with very high expectations for what college will be like. For example, about 9 in 10 expect that they will frequently: contribute to class discussions; apply what they are learning to other areas; incorporate information from outside the class into assignments and discussions; discuss different lifestyles; and interact with students from different backgrounds. They also expect to write a good deal, including essay exams. The portrait of the PPC-entering student is one who has a strong academic background and is highly involved in a variety of activities in high school; he expects to follow a similar path in college.

For more than a few, life at PPC does not measure up to their expectations. For example, though most did a fair amount of writing—about as much as they expected and far more than their peers at other types of institutions—44% never had an essay exam in the first year of college (Table 2.2). More than two fifths (44%) never socialized with their teachers outside of class, though most (93%) expected to do so at least occasionally, and they interacted much less often with peers with different views or religious backgrounds. At the same time, they often discussed ideas beyond the classroom with peers and faculty members. Taking ideas seriously here is modus operandi.

Table 2.2 Pristine Pond College Frequencies

		CSXQ	CSEQ
Contributing to class discussions	never	1%	1%
	occasionally	8%	22%
	frequently	91%	77%
Applying class material to other areas (job, relationships, etc.)	never	0%	3%
	occasionally	12%	29%
	frequently	88%	68%
Using a campus learning lab or center	never	13%	59%
	occasionally	61%	33%
	frequently	26%	8%
Becoming acquainted with students of different backgrounds	never	0%	1%
	occasionally	6%	20%
	frequently	94%	79%
Number of essays written	none	5%	44%
	fewer than 5	10%	14%
	between 5 and 10	34%	17%
	between 10 and 20	38%	16%
	more than 20	14%	10%
Student rating: Extent to which campus emphasizes diversity	Low (1,2)	1%	1%
	Middle (3,4,5)	16%	29%
	High (6,7)	83%	70%
Using information from other areas of life in class	never	0%	1%
	occasionally	10%	30%
	frequently	89%	69%
Discussing academic program with faculty	never	0%	2%
	occasionally	17%	39%
	frequently	83%	59%
Discussing career plans with faculty	never	2%	21%
	occasionally	33%	48%
	frequently	65%	31%
Socializing with faculty outside of class	never	7%	44%
	occasionally	63%	40%
	frequently	30%	16%

Table 2.2 continued

		CSXQ	CSEQ
Asking instructor about course performance	never	1%	28%
	occasionally	21%	39%
	frequently	79%	33%
Serious discussions with students having different political opinions	never	2%	19%
	occasionally	22%	51%
	frequently	75%	30%
Serious discussions with students of different religions	never	3%	15%
	occasionally	16%	42%
	frequently	81%	42%
Discussing different lifestyles, customs, and religions outside of class	never	1%	4%
	occasionally	9%	19%
	frequently	90%	77%
Discussing social/ethical issues related to science outside of class	never	3%	8%
	occasionally	25%	53%
	frequently	72%	39%

Despite the many good things happening on the Pristine Pond campus, the college wants to provide an even stronger learning and personal development experience for its students. The first step is to make sure that faculty and staff are aware of the high expectations PPC students have in terms of reading, writing, and interacting with faculty members.

The next step is to determine whether there are some areas where incoming students would benefit from learning more about what actually happens at PPC. For example, students expect to have a lot of informal contact with faculty outside the classroom. Undoubtedly, this is a signature appeal to prospective students. Admission materials and orientation activities could make it plain that students will often have to take the initiative in seeking out faculty members for informal conversation and socializing. It is also possible that while prior to college students think informal contact with faculty is something they want to pursue, they may later discover that they have sufficient contact with their instructors through, for example, the small, first-year seminar classes. Thus, while students' expectations for interacting with faculty may not necessarily be unrealistic, the range of their experiences with faculty members during the first year may offset any disappointment or potential negative impact on their learning and satisfaction. This seems to be the case at PPC as student satisfaction and the quality of relations with faculty are quite high, for example, compared with Western State College and University of the Great Plains described later. In any event, the nuances of what students expect from faculty and the meaning of their experiences with faculty at PPC need to be better understood, perhaps through focus groups with students.

There are other ways to increase student-faculty contact that can meet both students' affiliation and role modeling needs and serve faculty interests without requiring much more time from faculty. For example, an apprenticeship approach to doing research with a faculty member might be considered, as so many first-year PPC students desire such an experience. One way to do this is to assign an upper-division student who is working with a faculty member on a research project to be a peer mentor for two or three first-year students who wish to become involved, an approach used by some departments at Sweet Briar College and Wheaton College (Kuh, Kinzie, Schuh, Whitt, & Associates, 2005). This can have several positive outcomes: increased peer interaction in a substantive area; opportunities for upper-division students to gain experience by working with others in a tutoring role; and increased student-faculty contact.

Campus culture issues at PPC also need to be addressed. The reward system may warrant attention if it is determined that the amount of out-of-class student-faculty informal contact should increase. As indicated above, much more data are needed to confirm whether this is worth spending time on. The matter may be moot if students are, indeed, satisfied with their contacts with faculty and benefiting in the desired ways.

University of the Great Plains

The flagship institution of its state university system, the University of the Great Plains (UGP) is a large, public research institution. Classified as a doctoral/research-extensive institution, it is moderately selective (four on the Barron's scheme), and enrolls some 3,500 first-time, first-year students annually, the vast majority of whom are of traditional age and come from the home state. Its curriculum is broad and expansive, offering a wide range of undergraduate degree programs. As with many other research universities, UGP is grappling with how to balance its teaching and research missions, especially getting faculty to focus on improving undergraduate education.

True to the general pattern, UGP students expect more from their first college year than they get, though their expectations are not as uniformly high as, for example, those of their Pristine Pond College counterparts. For example, UGP students' expectations for interacting with faculty are relatively modest, more in line with what students at Western State College think will happen. Even so, far fewer UGP students come close to realizing these expectations when it comes to discussing with faculty their academic program, term papers, career plans, or academic performance (Table 2.3).

Most (84%) first-year students think they will in some way work with a faculty member on research, an opportunity UGP advances as a competitive advantage when courting prospective students because of the large number of faculty members who are actively pursuing research programs and scholarly activities. As Table 2.3 shows, these expectations are not realized by substantial numbers of UGP students. In addition, because most classes taken by first-year students are relatively large—many in excess of 150-200—instructors rely heavily on the lecture format, which tends to dampen active student involvement in class activities. For example, 85% of first-year students expected that they would frequently contribute to class discussions, but only 65% did so. Almost 90% thought they would frequently apply class material to other areas, but only half (52%) did so. At the same time, most students rate positively their relations with faculty, meaning they find them available, helpful, and sympathetic.

Table 2.3 University of the Great Plains Frequencies

		CSXQ	CSEQ
Contributing to class discussions	never	0%	1%
	occasionally	15%	35%
	frequently	85%	65%
Applying class material to other areas (job, relationships, etc.)	never	1%	7%
	occasionally	12%	41%
	frequently	87%	52%
Using a campus learning lab or center	never	11%	58%
	occasionally	53%	33%
	frequently	35%	9%
Becoming acquainted with students of different backgrounds	never	0%	1%
	occasionally	12%	33%
	frequently	87%	67%
Number of essays written	none	1%	12%
	fewer than 5	8%	41%
	between 5 and 10	31%	24%
	between 10 and 20	40%	17%
	more than 20	21%	6%
Student rating: Extent to which campus emphasizes diversity	Low (1,2)	2%	8%
	Middle (3,4,5)	54%	61%
	High (6,7)	44%	31%
Putting together different facts and ideas	never	0%	3%
	occasionally	10%	31%
	frequently	90%	65%

Table 2.3 continued

		CSXQ	CSEQ
Summarizing major points and information from class notes/readings	never	0%	5%
	occasionally	21%	35%
	frequently	79%	60%
Using information from other areas of life in class	never	1%	3%
	occasionally	15%	37%
	frequently	84%	60%
Working on projects that integrate ideas from various sources	never	0%	4%
	occasionally	17%	38%
	frequently	82%	59%
Asking instructors for course information (grades, assignments, etc.)	never	0%	4%
	occasionally	19%	46%
	frequently	80%	50%
Discussing academic program with faculty	never	1%	13%
	occasionally	36%	54%
	frequently	63%	33%
Discussing term paper or other class projects with faculty	never	2%	29%
	occasionally	46%	47%
	frequently	52%	24%
Working with faculty member on research	never	16%	76%
	occasionally	53%	14%
	frequently	30%	10%
Serious discussions with students having different personal values	never	2%	14%
	occasionally	31%	39%
	frequently	67%	47%
Serious discussions with students of different race	never	1%	25%
	occasionally	31%	48%
	frequently	68%	27%
Discussing social issues (peace, justice, etc.) outside of class	never	5%	10%
	occasionally	53%	52%
	frequently	41%	38%
Discussing different lifestyles, customs, and religions outside of class	never	2%	5%
	occasionally	51%	47%
	frequently	47%	48%
Student rating: Extent to which campus emphasizes vocational competence	Low (1,2)	2%	8%
	Middle (3,4,5)	49%	66%
	High (6,7)	50%	26%
Student rating: Extent to which campus emphasizes practical value of courses	Low (1,2)	1%	8%
	Middle (3,4,5)	47%	67%
	High (6,7)	52%	25%

Another systemic challenge facing UGP in terms of meeting students' expectations for the first college year is related to experiencing diversity. Virtually all students expect to interact, become acquainted, or have serious discussions with students from different racial and ethnic backgrounds. However, one quarter never do. In part, this is because UGP is not very structurally diverse; only 11% of undergraduates are from minority groups. It may also be because UGP faculty in general tend not to encourage students to bring in diverse perspectives in their courses or require readings and other assignments that draw on such material.

At big, organizationally complex campuses it is almost impossible to implement immediately effective educational practices on a large scale. Thus, the scope and focus of improvement efforts must be manageable. It's wise to focus on several programmatic interventions that have the potential to shrink the psychological size of the campus and positively influence student behaviors almost immediately.

At present, UGP does not require first-year students to either attend summer or fall orientation and registration events. Asking students to come to a summer program that is crafted and delivered well can give them a jump start on preparing for the academic demands of college. UGP should carefully consider how much time is needed to adequately introduce students to the campus environment and its academic activities, and perhaps even start a class early on in the process as part of its orientation activities.

Requiring students to live on campus the first year is another step that promises to increase student engagement. Research studies show that students who live on campus tend to be more involved in various academic and social activities and gain more from their college experience (Pascarella & Terenzini, 2005). They also are more likely to use the cultural and artistic venues the institution provides, interact more with faculty and other serious-minded peers, and have more experiences with diversity.

As described earlier in the Western State College example, introducing learning communities is another way to shrink the psychological size of a campus as well as increase student engagement. UGP could consider adding a residential component to some of its learning communities to form freshman interest groups comprised of students who live in close proximity and are taking some of the same classes together (Hossler, Kuh, & Olsen, 2001; Kuh, 2005).

Other initiatives to consider include guaranteeing that every first-year student would have at least one relatively small (25 students) discipline-based class taught by a seasoned instructor, something akin to what the University of Michigan did some years ago (Kuh, Kinzie, Schuh, Whitt & Associates, 2005). A variant of this is to add a required community service component to the small seminar or learning community.

Recall that far fewer UGP students use campus learning and support services than expect to. At a similar type of institution, Indiana University Bloomington, institutional research showed that students in high-risk courses were almost twice as likely to take advantage of help when it was available in their own residence hall as when the same service was provided in other campus locations. Indeed, when three academic skills centers were moved closer to where students lived, student use increased markedly. Equally important, those students who used the centers were more likely to persist to the second year and achieved slightly higher grades than students from similar backgrounds who did not seek academic skills tutoring (Hossler, et al., 2001).

As noted earlier, structural diversity—the number of students from different racial and ethnic backgrounds on campus—is important in creating the conditions for students to come into contact with people who are different from themselves. But it is not the most important or only factor for actually experiencing diversity. That is, just because students from different backgrounds attend an institution does not guarantee that they will interact in meaningful ways. Creating an institutional climate in which diversity is valued and encouraged is also essential. The climate for diversity represents students' perceptions that the institution encourages and values interaction among people from different backgrounds. Although UGP is not very structurally diverse, there are ways to incorporate diverse perspectives into the curriculum, thereby emphasizing the importance of diversity. This seems to be what many liberal arts colleges do that are located in rural areas and are not imbued with structural diversity. Yet, many of these institutions consistently score high on measures of experiencing diversity (Kuh & Umbach, 2005; Umbach & Kuh, in press). In addition, UGP could turn to the University of Michigan, the University of Maryland, Indiana University Bloomington, and Arizona State University to see first-hand how their innovative intergroup dialogues effectively bring together diverse groups of students to discuss substantive issues with desired benefits (Schoem & Hurtado, 2001).

Atlantic County Community College

Located on the fringe of a major urban area on the eastern seaboard, Atlantic County Community College (ACCC) enrolls more than 20,000 students on three campuses within the county. More than a third of the students are 25 years of age or older, with about 55% attending school part-time. Almost one third are students of color. It offers a wide range of degree and certificate programs, including business; communications and the arts; health, education, and human services; liberal arts and sciences; and computer studies, engineering, and technology. Starting with less than a dozen full-time faculty members in 1961, ACCC is now staffed by more than 400 full-time faculty augmented by 1,000 adjunct instructors. Many special-learning opportunities exist, including honors programs; English as a second language; numerous co-ops and internships; programs for returning adult students; joint admissions agreements with many baccalaureate-granting institutions in the state; co-curricular activities; and a wide range of student services including child care on each of the three campuses. True to its mission of bringing postsecondary educational opportunity to everyone in its cache, ACCC practices open admissions, and classes are offered at four nearby high schools. Also, its distance education offerings are expanding rapidly.

Two things stand out about the expectations and experiences of ACCC students (Table 2.4). First, their expectations for engaging in various activities are somewhat lower in many areas compared with their counterparts attending four-year schools. In part, this may be because of the great variations in students' age and academic interests, and the fact that many more ACCC students attend college part-time; thus, because they are on campus less time per week, they have fewer opportunities to interact with others or participate in certain activities. For example, while at least 85% of students at UGP and PPC expected to frequently contribute to class discussions and apply class material to other areas of their lives, only two thirds to three quarters of ACCC students thought they would do so. In a few areas, however, such as asking instructors for course information and discussing the academic program with faculty, students' expectations are quite similar across two-year and four-year settings, suggesting that what students want from faculty is pretty consistent—age and enrollment status notwithstanding.

Table 2.4 Atlantic County Community College Frequencies

		CSXQ	CSEQ
Contributing to class discussions	never	4%	3%
	occasionally	29%	26%
	frequently	67%	72%
Applying class material to other areas (job, relationships, etc.)	never	1%	8%
	occasionally	22%	27%
	frequently	77%	65%
Using a campus learning lab or center	never	13%	29%
	occasionally	41%	27%
	frequently	46%	44%
Becoming acquainted with students of different backgrounds	never	3%	9%
	occasionally	27%	35%
	frequently	70%	56%

Table 2.4 continued

		CSXQ	CSEQ
Number of essays written	none	4%	10%
	fewer than 5	16%	32%
	between 5 and 10	37%	35%
	between 10 and 20	43%	16%
	more than 20	0%	7%
Student rating: Extent to which campus emphasizes diversity	Low (1,2)	100%	57%
	Middle (3,4,5)	0%	43%
	High (6,7)	0%	0%
Using information from other areas of life in class	never	2%	6%
	occasionally	24%	27%
	frequently	74%	68%
Working on projects integrating ideas from various sources	never	2%	4%
	occasionally	27%	26%
	frequently	71%	69%
Asking instructor for course information (grades, assignments, etc.)	never	2%	4%
	occasionally	19%	35%
	frequently	80%	61%
Discussing academic program with faculty	never	4%	15%
	occasionally	33%	43%
	frequently	62%	43%
Discussing term paper or other class projects with faculty	never	6%	22%
	occasionally	37%	37%
	frequently	58%	41%
Serious discussions with students of different race	never	11%	21%
	occasionally	33%	35%
	frequently	57%	43%
Discussing current events in the news outside of class	never	5%	3%
	occasionally	36%	25%
	frequently	59%	72%
Discussing social issues (peace, justice, etc.) outside of class	never	7%	8%
	occasionally	44%	36%
	frequently	49%	56%
Discussing different lifestyles, customs, and religions outside of class	never	7%	8%
	occasionally	40%	36%
	frequently	53%	56%
Student rating: Extent to which campus emphasizes academics and scholarship	never	96%	57%
	occasionally	4%	43%
	frequently	0%	0%

The second point worth noting is that while ACCC students expect to be less engaged, they generally come closer to realizing their expectations in some areas—and even exceed them in a few. For example, only two thirds of ACCC students expected to frequently contribute to class discussions, but 72% reported actually doing so. One explanation may be that instructors at ACCC organize discussions in ways that essentially require students to at least occasionally participate; perhaps the grading structures in some classes even require students to participate. It is also possible that the recent systemic general education revision that emphasized the use of active and collaborative teaching approaches is having a demonstrable impact.

Another area where ACCC students' experiences outpace their expectations is with regard to the emphasis they think the institution will place on experiencing diversity. Surprisingly, none of the students before they started taking classes at ACCC thought the school would emphasize the educational importance of diversity beyond a minimal level. By the end of the first year, however, more than two fifths (43%) recognized that the college was, indeed, serious about this important area. One thing ACCC could consider is reviewing its Web site, admission materials, and other public documents to see if the college emphasizes the educational value of diversity plainly enough to prospective students and the public at large. Orientation programs and materials also should be revisited with the same purpose in mind.

As with students at the other institutions, a sizeable fraction (29%) of ACCC students never uses campus learning labs or centers. This is so despite assigning each student a faculty academic advisor and making available tutorial services and learning labs for mathematics, computers, reading, and writing. Although ACCC publicizes the existence of these services, it could consider redoubling its efforts and paying heed to Turner's (1998) admonition reported earlier—instructors and other staff need to periodically remind students of these opportunities and occasionally even cajole students into using them. In some instances, requiring the use of tutoring or writing and math-learning labs may be appropriate.

ACCC students expect to have much more contact with their teachers than they do. Although a similar pattern exists at other types of institutions, because so many ACCC students attend part-time and commute to campus, the importance of the classroom to student success increases in magnitude. On residential campuses, peers are—for better or worse—readily available to help answer questions, and faculty and advisors are easier to contact. At ACCC, virtually all of the social as well as academic needs of students must be addressed in some fashion in the classroom, the one point of contact all students have on a regular basis with the institution. Thus, ACCC may wish to devote some time to creating and implementing a series of faculty and staff development initiatives that demonstrate how the classroom can be used effectively as the primary locus for student learning and community building (Roueche, Ely, & Roueche, 2001).

Another intervention that ACCC might consider to increase student-faculty and student-student interactions and experiences with diversity is experimenting with alternative forms of learning communities tailored for the types of students ACCC enrolls. One such model is that developed at Skagit Valley College in Washington which offers annually about 70 learning communities involving more than half of the full-time faculty and many part-time instructors from almost all academic departments and programs (Dunlap & Stanwood, 2003). Other variants of learning communities adaptable to ACCC are at Seattle Central Community College (Finley, 1990) and La Guardia Community College (Mathews, Cooper, Davidson, & Hawkes, 1995) among other places (MacGregor & Smith, 2005).

Implications

Helping students and institutions set and hold one another accountable for realizing reasonable expectations is a complex, multifaceted, mutually shaping process that is evolving continually. Indeed, "Student expectations are a moving target" (Kuh, Kinzie, Schuh, & Whitt, 2005, p. 60). Every year, upwards of one third of the undergraduates at four-year colleges are new to the institution. This number may swell to half or more at two-year institutions. So, every year a college must, beginning long before newcomers arrive, clearly communicate what students should be ready and able to do, and then present students with sufficient academic challenges and support to help them adjust and thrive in college, both academically and socially. After students arrive, the first six to eight weeks of the first semester are thought to be especially important. During this period, students are forming impressions about the university environment and habits that will dictate how much they will engage in the activities that matter to their learning (Pascarella & Terenzini, 2005; Tinto, 1993; Upcraft, et al., 2005).

Faculty members and student affairs professionals are integral to giving students signals about whether they are allocating their time appropriately. There is no substitute for frequent feedback during these early weeks of school to improve a student's chances for success in the first college year.

The initiatives suggested earlier for fully engaging more students more frequently are not panaceas. But, when designed to complement the institution's mission and tailored to students' characteristics, they have the potential to improve the first-year experience. As with any educational program or practice, these initiatives must be implemented at a high level of quality. That is, it is not enough to simply provide as many programs and activities as possible and hope for the best. Too often, such efforts fall far short of the desired levels of both quality and participation. Rather, the goal is to stitch those initiatives together in complementary ways and scale up those that have proven to be educationally effective to a point where virtually every student is touched in some meaningful way by one or more (Kuh, Kinzie, Schuh, Whitt, & Associates, 2005).

Student Expectations

Now, we offer sets of questions and discussion points to help those who are gathering information about student expectations on individual campuses. Each section summarizes some of the data and research regarding student expectations in that area, and then suggests research questions to be explored. Finally, we suggest some discussion questions that can be used to query the information a campus has about its students' expectations and experiences. In combination with other resources (Kuh, Kinzie, Schuh, & Whitt, 2005; Miller, et al., 2005), colleges and universities can use these ideas to stimulate discussion and further exploration and understanding of student expectations on their own campuses.

Learning and the Academic Environment

The indications:

Learning for its own sake is not a widely held value of the current cohort of college students. Instead there is a substantial focus on career relevance and the relationship between the academic experience and the employability of the student. The concern of students for curricular relevance has an impact on their receptivity to general education and core curriculum courses.

Some students have romantic notions about faculty interest in their lives, while others are indifferent to developing relationships with faculty. Some institutions value highly the faculty-mentoring relationship with students, while others focus less on undergraduate learning. The match between the expectation of the student and the academic culture of the institution is not always perfect.

The extent to which students are ready for college-level learning warrants attention. Most campuses have one or more groups of students who are underprepared. As a result, substantial proportions are assigned to developmental education programs, which are expected to close the gap between the current and the ideal student learning skills. The outcome of those programs may be inconsistent with the student expectation of them. For example, if students think that developmental course work will enable them to work less hard or spend less time on their learning challenges, they might be disappointed.

Many students expect to realize more academic success than they will have. Their expectations of the amount of time and effort they will devote to academics are relatively accurate, but their grades tend to be lower than they had expected. Further, the amount of time they spend on academic work is substantially less than what faculty would suggest is necessary.

Campus assessment issues:

Have data about student expectations regarding the academic experience been collected? What do incoming students expect regarding their own performance? How realistic are those expectations? How much time is spent by students on academic work as compared to what they expect to spend? How does it compare with what faculty members suggest? Are campus developmental education programs effective?

Are there student subgroups with special performance issues? Do transfer students perform at the same level as native students? Athletes? Commuting students? First-generation students? Students with families? What are the subgroups that merit academic support?

What is known about student experiences with the academic program? Is there much shifting of majors? From what disciplines to what others? What is known about the reasons behind student choices of major? How do prior experiences, particularly for adult students, affect major and performance expectations?

How are relationships between students and faculty characterized by students? By faculty? How do those relationships compare with what students anticipate at entry?

Points to ponder:

- If there is dissonance between the expectations of students regarding their academic performance and their actual experiences, what needs to be done about that?
- How can students be better informed to anticipate the nature and rigors of academic work in college?
- What are the inhibitors to student performance?
- How does performance relate to major?
- If there is dissonance between student expectations about their relationships with faculty and their real experiences, what should be done?

- Is this a matter of changing the expectation and better informing students about the likely nature of their relationships with faculty, or is it a matter of trying to change the actual quality of the relationship?
- Are there differences in this issue across disciplines?
- Are there differences by student subgroups, and, if so, how might that be addressed?

College Life and Campus Environment

The indications:

Evidence suggests that students often have different out-of-class experiences than they had anticipated. However, having social success appears to be a high priority for students, especially at four-year colleges, so they invest a significant amount of energy in making friends and fitting in.

There are subsets of the student population with specific and special expectations. Student-athletes, particularly males, are brimming with self-confidence, and anticipate success in athletics, academics, and their social lives. Students expecting to participate in Greek-letter organizations also have a high level of social confidence and related expectations for success.

Students living in residence halls have high expectations for that environment and the college experience in general. Students with disabilities may have expectations derived from school experiences that may not be met in higher education.

The special interests of adult students differ sharply from those of traditional age students, and ways in which they engage campus life are similarly different.

Students are generally keenly interested in community service and volunteer activity, but they might not act on that interest as much as they think they will.

Perhaps related to academic performance expectations, the incidence of academic misconduct is higher than students expect.

The diversity in higher education is different than students expect, but, after the freshman year, many students report fewer experiences with persons not like them as they gravitate to interaction with others who share the same traits in race, ethnicity, religious orientations, and so forth (Kuh, 2003). This is the case, even though experiences with diversity are predictive of student success. A growing proportion of college students come from home environments where languages other than English are spoken. These differences lead to complex student expectations.

Campus assessment issues:

What are student expectations for campus life, and how closely do they approximate the real experiences of students? What are the particular expectations of significant student subgroups like athletes, fraternity and sorority members, adult students, students with disabilities, first-generation students, commuting students, and those of different ethnic groups?

How closely do student messages about college life match the messages found in campus publications and advertising? How do messages found in campus publications and advertising influence student expectations for the campus experience?

What are student expectations regarding diversity and how closely do they match with campus reality?

What is the relationship between campus climate and student outcomes regarding perceptions of diversity? How do student views about diversity change as a result of attendance at the institution?

Points to ponder:

- If there is a difference between student expectations for campus life and the realities, what needs to be done about that?
- Is it a matter for better communication about campus life to generate accurate expectations, or is it a matter of changing the quality and nature of campus life to meet existing expectations?
- Are there data that document how students might expect to change when attending the university? If so, how might this be utilized to help students form accurate expectations of their college experience?
- Are there student subgroups with special needs associated with their expectations, and, if so, how should they be addressed?

Student Services

The indications:

Partly due to continued increases in college costs, students and parents have high expectations about the return on their investment in a college education. Many of the expectations students hold center around the services that will be provided and the efficiency and effectiveness surrounding the delivery of these services. Key characteristics of the expectations of students regarding services have to do with convenience and timeliness.

Students might not be invested highly in a particular student service until they have a need for it. When they do have a transaction to conduct, they expect to do it easily, conveniently, and quickly.

Campus assessment issues:

What do assessment measures show about student perceptions of services? Is there a convenient flow to student services and prompt delivery of them? Is technology used appropriately to enhance service delivery? What do assessment measures show about the utilization of services? Are there groups of students who overutilize or underutilize student services?

Points to ponder:

- If there is evidence that students are not satisfied with student services, what needs to be done to improve the circumstances?

- Are promotional materials accurately representing the services students may expect?

- Is there a clear mission statement that informs students what they might gain from attendance at the institution?

- How do we communicate to students the educational goals that exist within the university, and how might this affect their experiences with a variety of services on campus?

- How do the services provided complement the academic mission?

- If services are underutilized, how should this condition be addressed?

- What can be enhanced immediately, and what longer-range plans can be established?

- Are there differences among subgroups regarding the expectations, utilization, or satisfaction with campus services?

College Expenses

The indications:

A substantial proportion of current students hold part-time jobs during college, and many even have full-time jobs. This seems to be the result of the cost of college attendance and the desire to make it affordable. However, there are also lifestyle issues, and students make choices to purchase material things, and they spend a fair amount of money on things not directly related to their educational experiences. Evidence suggests that the cost of college attendance is rising much more rapidly than family incomes. Fewer families are taking loans to cover the costs of college, but those who are borrowing are taking on larger debt than before.

When students and parents are asked to estimate the cost of a college education, they typically overestimate this amount. At the same time, the willingness of families to save for college does not reflect this expectation of inflated cost. Parents are typically unwilling to go into debt to fund their children's education. The tendency is to shift the burden of debt for college to the student through the use of low-interest federal loans. An increasing proportion of families attach student performance expectations, like a certain academic grade point average, to their willingness to provide financial support to students.

The poor are particularly challenged by circumstances besides income levels. Parents' familiarity with financial aid processes and financial planning for college is closely related to socioeconomic status.

Campus assessment issues:

To what extent is cost associated with persistence issues on campus? What decisions do students make regarding paying those costs, and how are work and loans balanced with financial aid grants and self-help? How is information about cost conveyed to students and families? How frequently in the recent past has cost of attendance exceeded the consumer price index? How accurate are prospective students' and parents' expectations regarding the cost of college?

Points to ponder:

- How are students and families informed about initial cost and also about changes in costs?

- How far in advance are cost increases announced to families?

- What strategies are employed when cost of attendance rises faster than inflation, and how is affordability maintained in those circumstances?

- If expectations regarding cost are significantly off-target, how can accurate information be shared with families?

Persistence and Educational Attainment

The indications:

The overwhelming proportion of students entering four-year institutions reflects the intention to graduate within four years. Few indicate that they plan to drop out or transfer to another institution (Sax et. al., 2002). However, fewer graduate within four years (or at all) than plan to (Astin & Oseguera, 2002). A large portion of students attending two-year institutions are less committed to degree attainment, with different objectives associated with their enrollment (Berkner, He, & Cataldi, 2002). Transfer students as a group are less engaged in educational activities and campus life (Kuh, 2003).

When viewing persistence through the lens of student expectations, one might suggest that much of attrition may be related to unmet expectations. The cognitive dissonance that is created when reality compares unfavorably to expectations may lead some to drop out (Howard, 2005).

Campus assessment issues:

If campus assessment reflects a rate of persistence that is lower than expected or than predicted by students, what are the contributing factors? To what extent can attrition be predicted and intervention strategies designed? What is known about the destinations of students who leave?

How are transfer students engaged, and are they persisting at an acceptable rate? What is known about reasons for attrition? What do exit surveys show about unmet expectations? How do persistence rates vary by student subgroups? What factors account for the variation?

Points to ponder:

• If persistence rates are less than desired or expected, what are the remedies?

• Do they relate to better informing students so as to affect their expectations?

• Alternatively, what are the solutions associated with improving institutional performance in predicting attrition and intervening with retention-related activities and programs?

• Are the students recruited to the institution best suited for success there?

Outcomes

The indications:

Many of the outcomes of the college experience are associated with student expectations. Students expect to attain worthwhile degrees, they expect to have the opportunity for graduate study, and they expect to be employable. Students expect to learn while in college, and they expect to develop the leadership and interpersonal skills they will need to succeed.

Many students attending colleges do not expect to attain degrees, but have a specific employment-related purpose or goals related to personal growth and enrichment.

There are other outcomes of a college education that students might not have expected. The social benefits of education include that college graduates are more involved in the educational experiences of their children; they are more apt to run for public office and to exercise their citizenship right to vote; they are more apt to volunteer in their communities; they are healthier; and they have more stable marriages.

Campus assessment issues:

What is known about what students at your campus expect to learn while in college? How do they expect to change and grow? What do they want to be able to do when they graduate? Of those students expecting to attend graduate and professional schools, what portion of them does so upon graduation? Of students attending community colleges expecting to transfer to four-year schools, what portion of them fulfill this expectation? Of students expecting to enter or advance in the employment market, what portion of them does so successfully?

How do student-learning expectations match up with measured and demonstrated learning?

What are the other outcomes of the student experience and how are they measured?

What does/can the institution do to expand student expectations about what can be accomplished through their student experience?

Points to ponder:

- If the plans of students regarding the postcollege experience are not consistent with the actual outcomes, why is that the case?

- Is there some action that the institution should consider due to any dissonance in this issue?

- Are students less likely to proceed immediately to graduate and professional programs than they originally believed? If so, why? What, if anything, should be done?

- Are the employment-related outcomes consistent with student expectations? If not, why? What, if anything, should be done?

- If there are other significant outcomes associated with the student experience, are those outcomes consistent with the mission and purpose of the institution?

- If they are unexpected by students, should something be done to inform incoming students about them?

Expectations of Other Constituents

Many colleges and universities spend substantial amounts of time, money, and energy trying to meet the expectations of other constituencies such as parents, alumni, employers, and the broader community. At times, these expectations may conflict with student expectations, and compromises must be sought. For example, communities may seek roles for the institution in governing student conduct off-campus that conflict with what students expect. The assessment of the expectations of these groups must be done separately and differently than the assessment of students. Much of this assessment will be informal and gathered through conversations, interactions, and various forms of communication with these constituents. Also instructive may be surveys of parents, alumni, and employers. As mentioned in the previous discussion of assessment strategies, gathering data without wide institutional support and plans for dissemination accomplishes little. In this section, we present no specific campus assessment issues, as institutional circumstances vary greatly. Institutions should craft their assessment strategies about external constituents around the unique context in which they exist. Some of the questions that may be appropriate for universities to ask each of these interest groups are addressed in the following section.

Parents and Families

The indications:

There is evidence that families have an increasing level of interest in the college experiences of students (Hoover, 2004). Parents are paying close attention to the interaction between their sons and daughters and the colleges they attend. Many parents base their expectations for college performance on their own experiences, which may or may not have a direct bearing on institutional performance.

Many parents are highly involved in helping their student choose a college, actively participating in, and sometimes heavily influencing, the final choice.

Not all family issues are those of parents of students. Almost one quarter of students in higher education have dependents, with female students having more.

Points to ponder:

- How does the institution interact with parents of students?

- How much and in what manner are parents engaged as a constituency?

- If there is more to accomplish regarding the understanding of and response to parent expectations, what needs to be addressed?

- If a substantial portion of students are, themselves, parents, what accommodations are provided to the student-parent, and is it satisfactory?

Communities and Local Government

The indications:

For many reasons, the public has a growing interest in and involvement with higher education. For many campuses, relationships with the communities and neighborhoods in which their campuses exist are laden with expectations for institutional performance, some of which are quite challenging. Students living in residential communities surrounded by owner-occupied homes may find themselves perceived as unwelcome intruders.

Community colleges, of course, exist to serve the communities of which they are a part, but some expectations held by the public can present difficulties for institutions. Those expectations may relate to parking issues, traffic problems, or the conduct of students as it relates to the community.

Points to ponder:

- How is the institutional relationship with the immediate community characterized? If the relationship should be improved, what needs to be done, by whom, and how?

- What relationships does the institution have with local government?

- How broadly are campus constituents involved with government representatives?

- Who is responsible for monitoring campus interests in local public policy, and how broadly do those individuals engage the campus community?

- Are the relationships with government used to the advantage of the institution? How could they be improved and enhanced?

- How do the policies and practices of local law enforcement officials influence social activities and student experiences on and off campus?

Alumni and Donors

The indications:

Graduates have been actively engaged in the affairs of their alma maters for many generations. Virtually all institutions have created staff positions to foster relationships with alumni. There have been many occasions when alumni have been aggressive in their expressions of interest in institutional affairs, creating difficult circumstances for colleges. Alumni fraternity members who become involved in discipline matters may not be sympathetic to the institution's interests, or athletic team boosters may become involved in sports matters that compromise the image of the institution.

Donors express their interests in institutions through their generous benefactions. The vast majority of those donors have gracefully and generously made gifts free of special requirements. However, there have also been occasions when donors have established challenging expectations for institutional performance.

Points to ponder:

- How does the institution manage alumni affairs in the context of student welfare and interests?
- To what extent are alumni engaged in institutional decision making and how is their input managed?
- How do alumni interests affect the student experience, and are there ways in which that impact should change?
- How are donor expectations generated, and how does the institution manage them?
  Are there ways in which donor interests are in conflict with institutional values?
- Do donor interests adversely impact the student/institutional relationship?
- How does the institution manage alumni reactions to changes in campus traditions, culture, policies, and practices?

Employers

The indications:

There are many ways in which employer expectations of institutions may be unmet, given the amount of time and resources dedicated to employee training and skill building. That commitment by employers to further educate staff applies to many walks of life, from the business fields to the teaching profession to technological fields. Some of this may relate to quality improvement issues for employers or lifelong learning for individuals, but it may also be related to some perceived limitation of the effect of college education, or at least the lack of acquisition by graduates of necessary skills and knowledge.

Points to ponder:

• What does the institution know about the perceptions and expectations of employers regarding graduates?

• What is the evidence regarding alumni persistence and advancement in their employment?

• What does the institution know—and do—about alumni perceptions of their own preparedness for the world of work?

Conclusion

If this guide is of help to campus administrators in their study of the expectations of students and how their actual experiences compare and contrast with those expectations, the authors will have satisfied their objectives. Used in concert with the material in *Promoting Reasonable Expectations*, it may help administrators make decisions that result in improved relationships with students. We provided examples of institutions that have used the study of student expectations and the contrast of those expectations with real experiences. Those examples illustrate the usefulness of understanding student expectations. Campuses are encouraged to use this guide to inform and support campus discussions about student expectations, the college experience, institutional assessment potential, and ways in which the relationships between institutions and the students they enroll can be enhanced and improved.

The most effective use of these principles will be based broadly and will engage wide segments of campus communities. Using assessment information about student expectations and actual student experiences, powerful arguments can be made for faculty, students, and institutional leadership to engage the areas of dissonance and use them to effect change in policies and practices.

The authors invite those who have studied student expectations and used the results to effect campus changes in policy and practice to report their experiences to us. We will compile application efforts and track the uses of results to further inform practice. Those wishing to share their experiences are invited to write to the authors in care of:

Thomas E. Miller
Division of Student Affairs
University of South Florida
4202 E. Fowler Ave. ADM151
Tampa, FL 33620

References

American Association of University Professors. (1968). *Joint statement on rights and freedoms of students.* Washington, DC: American Association of University Professors.

Arnold, K., & Kuh, G.D. (1999). What matters in undergraduate education? Mental models, student learning, and student affairs. In E.J. Whitt (Ed.), *Student learning as student affairs work: Responding to our imperative* (pp. 11-34). Washington, DC: National Association of Student Personnel Administrators.

Astin, A. W. (1993). *What matters in college? Four critical years revisited.* San Francisco: Jossey-Bass.

Astin A.W., & Oseguera, L. (2002). *Degree attainment rates at American colleges and universities.* Los Angeles: University of California, Higher Education Research Institute.

College Division of Barron's Educational Series (Ed.). (2002). *Barron's profiles of American colleges* (23rd ed.). Hauppauge, NY: Barron's Educational Series.

Center for Postsecondary Research. (2005). *The Beginning College Survey of Student Engagement 2005-2006.* Bloomington, IN: Indiana University.

Berkner, L., He, S., & Cataldi, E.F. (2002). *Descriptive summary of 1995-96 beginning postsecondary students: Six years later* (NCES 2003151). Washington, DC: U.S. Department of Education, National Center for Education Statistics

Braxton, J., Hossler, D., & Vesper, N. (1995). Incorporating college choice constructs into Tinto's model of student departure: Fulfillment of expectations for institutional traits and student withdrawal plans. *Research in Higher Education,* 36 (5), 595-612.

Dungy, G.J., Rissmeyer, P.A., & Roberts, G. (2005). The influence of selected students' characteristics on their expectations of college. In T. Miller, B. Bender, J. Schuh, & Associates, *Promoting reasonable expectations: Aligning student and institutional views of the college experience* (pp. 175-189). San Francisco: Jossey-Bass.

Dunlap, L., & Stanwood, L. (2003). The assessment chase: The changing shape of assessment in shaping change at Skagit Valley College. In J. MacGregor (Ed.), *Doing learning community assessment: Five campus stories.* National Learning Communities Project Monograph Series. Olympia, WA: The Evergreen State College, Washington Center for Improving the Quality of Undergraduate Education.

Finley, N.J. (1990). Meeting expectations by making new connections: Curriculum reform at Seattle Central. *Educational Record, 71*(4), 50-53.

Hoover, E. (2004, January 16). Parents united. *Chronicle of Higher Education*, p. A23.

Hossler, D., Kuh, G.D., & Olsen, D. (2001). Finding fruit on the vines: Using higher education research and institutional research to guide institutional policies and strategies. (Part II) *Research in Higher Education, 42,* 223-235.

Howard, J.A. (2005). Why should we care about student expectations? In T. Miller, B. Bender, J. Schuh, & Associates, *Promoting reasonable expectations: Aligning student and institutional views of the college experience* (pp. 10-33). San Francisco: Jossey-Bass.

Hu, S., & Kuh, G.D. (2003). Diversity experiences and college student learning and personal development. *Journal of College Student Development, 44,* 320-334.

Hurtado, S., Milem, J., Clayton-Pedersen, A., & Allen, W. (1999). *Enacting diverse learning environments: Improving the climate for racial/ethnic diversity in higher education.* Washington, DC: The George Washington University.

Kelly, G. (1955*). The psychology of personal constructs.* New York: Norton.

Kuh, G.D. (1999). Setting the bar high to promote student learning. In G.S. Blimling, E.J. Whitt, & Associates, *Good practice in student affairs: Principles to foster student learning.* San Francisco: Jossey-Bass.

Kuh, G.D. (2003). What we're learning about student engagement from NSSE. *Change, 35*(2), 24-32.

Kuh, G. D. (2005). *National Survey of Student Engagement 2006: The College Student Report.* Bloomington, IN: Indiana University.

Kuh, G.D. (2005). Student engagement in the first year of college. In Upcraft, L.M., Gardner, J.N., & Barefoot, B.O. (Eds.), *Meeting challenges and building support: Creating a climate for first-year student success.* San Francisco: Jossey-Bass.

Kuh, G.D., Gonyea, R. M., & Williams, J. M. (2005). What students expect from college and what they get. In T. Miller, B. Bender, J. Schuh, & Associates, *Promoting reasonable expectations: Aligning student and institutional views of the college experience* (pp. 34-64). San Francisco: Jossey-Bass.

Kuh, G.D., Kinzie, J., Schuh, J.H., Whitt, E.J., & Associates (2005). *Student success in college: Creating conditions that matter.* San Francisco: Jossey-Bass.

Kuh, G.D., Kinzie, J., Schuh, J.H., & Whitt, E.J. (2005). *Assessing conditions to enhance educational effectiveness: The Inventory for Student Engagement and Success.* San Francisco: Jossey-Bass.

Kuh, G.D., Nelson Laird, T.F., & Umbach, P.D. (2004). Aligning faculty and student behavior: Realizing the promise of Greater Expectations. *Liberal Education, 90*(4), 24-31.

Kuh, G. D., & Pace, C. R. (1999). *College student expectations questionnaire* (2nd ed.). Bloomington, IN: Indiana University Center for Postsecondary Research.

Kuh, G.D., & Umbach, P.D. (2005). Experiencing diversity: What can we learn from liberal arts colleges? *Liberal Education, 91*(1), 14-21.

Levine, A., & Cureton, J.S. (1998). Collegiate life: An obituary. *Change, 30*(3), 12-17, 51.

MacGregor, J., & Smith, B.L. (2005). Where are learning communities now: National leaders take stock. *About Campus, 10*(2), 2-8.

Matthews, R.S., Cooper, J.L., Davidson, N., & Hawkes, P. (1995). Building bridges between cooperative and collaborative learning. *Change, 27*(4), 35-40.

McCormick, A.C. (Ed.). (2001). The Carnegie classification of institutions of higher education, 2000 edition. Menlo Park, CA: The Carnegie Foundation for the Advancement of Teaching.

Miller, T. E. (2005). Introduction. In T. Miller, B. Bender, J. Schuh, & Associates, *Promoting reasonable expectations: Aligning student and institutional views of the college experience* (pp. 1-9). San Francisco: Jossey-Bass.

Miller, T.E., Bender, B.E., Schuh, J.H., & Associates, (2005). *Promoting reasonable expectations: Aligning student and institutional views of the college experience.* San Francisco: Jossey-Bass.

National Association of Student Personnel Administrators (1994). *Reasonable expectations.* Washington, DC: National Association of Student Personnel Administrators.

National Survey of Student Engagement (2001). *Improving the college experience: National benchmarks for effective educational practice.* Bloomington, IN: Indiana University Center for Postsecondary Research.

Olsen, D., Kuh, G. D., Schilling, K.M., Schilling, K., Connolly, M., Simmons, A., et al. (November 1998). *Great expectations: What students expect from college and what they get.* Paper presented at the annual meeting of the Association for the Study of Higher Education, Miami, FL.

Pace, C. R., & Kuh, G. D. (1998). *College student experiences questionnaire* (4th ed.). Bloomington, IN: Indiana University Center for Postsecondary Research.

Pascarella, E. T., & Terenzini, P. T. (2005). *How college affects students: A third decade of research* (Vol. 2). San Francisco: Jossey-Bass.

Roueche, J.E., Ely, E.E., & Roueche, S.D. (2001). *In pursuit of excellence: The Community College of Denver*. Washington, DC: Community College Press, American Association of Community Colleges.

Rousseau, D.M. (1995). *Psychological contracts in organizations*. Thousand Oaks, CA: Sage.

Sax, L.J., Lindholm, J.A., Astin, A.W., Korn, W.S., & Mahoney, K.M. (2002). *The American freshman: National norms for fall 2002*. Los Angeles: Higher Education Research Institute.

Schoem, D. L., & Hurtado, S. (Eds.). (2001). *Intergroup dialogue: Deliberative democracy in school, college, community, and workplace*. Ann Arbor, MI: University of Michigan Press.

Taylor, K., with Moore, S. MacGregor, J., & Lindblad, J. (2003). *Learning community research and assessment: What we know now*. National Learning Communities Project Monograph Series. Olympia, WA: The Evergreen State College, Washington Center for Improving the Quality of Undergraduate Education.

Tinto, V. (1993). *Leaving college: Rethinking the causes and cures of student attrition* (2nd ed.). Chicago: University of Chicago Press.

Tinto, V. (2000). What have we learned about the impact of learning communities on students? *Assessment Update, 12*, 1-2, 12.

Turner, R.C. (1998). *Teaching English to another generation of students*. Unpublished manuscript.

Umbach, P.D., & Kuh, G.D. (in press). Student experiences with diversity at liberal arts colleges: Another claim for distinctiveness. *Journal of Higher Education*.

Upcraft, M.L., Gardner, J.N., Barefoot, B.O., & Associates (2005). *Challenging and supporting the first-year student: A handbook for improving the first year of college*. San Francisco: Jossey-Bass.

Zhao, C-M., & Kuh, G.D. (2004). Adding value: Learning communities and student engagement. *Research in Higher Education, 45*, 115-138.